KU-639-919

Contents

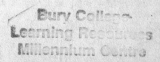

Introduction

Samantha Sanders was nine years old when she found Alvin Howell – dead.

Sam lives by the Powhatan Swamp, in Carolina. She can't forget that day when she was nine, when she found the dead man. Seven years later, she goes back into the swamp and stays there for a night. She is very afraid. Then she meets 'The Weirdo' – a boy, called Chip. After that, nothing is the same again . . .

Theodore Taylor is an American writer. He was born in North Carolina in 1921. Now he lives in California with his family. His most famous book is called *The Cay*. *The Cay* is also a Penguin Reader.

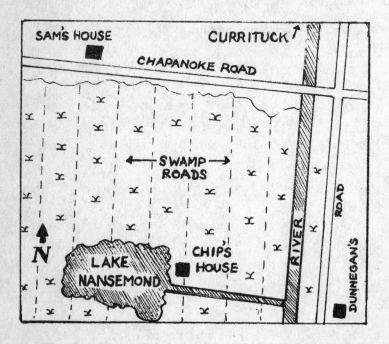

The Weirdo

THEODORE TAYLOR

Level 2

Retold by Diane Hall
Series Editors: Andy Hopkins and Jocelyn Potter

Pearson Education Limited
Edinburgh Gate, Harlow,
Essex CM20 2JE, England
and Associated Companies throughout the world.

ISBN 0 582 41679 5

First published in Great Britain by Viking 1994
This adaptation first published by Penguin Books 1996
Published by Addison Wesley Longman Limited and Penguin Books Ltd. 1998
New edition first published 1999

Second impression 2000

Text copyright © Diane Hall 1996
Illustrations copyright © Kay Dixey 1996
All rights reserved

The moral right of the adapter and of the illustrator has been asserted

Typeset by Digital Type, London
Set in 11/14pt Bembo
Printed in Spain by Mateu Cromo, S. A. Pinto (Madrid)

Published by Pearson Education Limited in association with
Penguin Books Ltd, both companies being subsidiaries of Pearson Plc

For a complete list of the titles available in the Penguin Readers series please write to your local
Pearson Education office or to: Marketing Department, Penguin Longman Publishing,
5 Bentinck Street, London W1M 5RN.

Chapter 1 1982

Samantha Sanders was nine years old when she found Alvin Howell – dead. When she arrived home from school that afternoon she saw something blue in the swamp. She left her books at the front door and went to look at the blue thing in the swamp. When she got there, she saw a man's face, mouth open, eyes open and afraid. There was some red on his blue shirt.

Samantha started to cry. She ran back to the house and phoned her mother, Dell, at her office in Currituck.

'Mum, Mum . . . there's a dead man!'

'Where, Samantha?'

'Dead man . . .'

'Where, Samantha? Tell me, slowly, now.'

'In front of the house, in the swamp . . .'

'OK. Listen. I'll phone the police. Stay in the house. I'll get there as quickly as I can.'

Dell arrived home twenty minutes later, before the policeman, Ed Truesdale, arrived from Currituck. He went to look at the body in the swamp and then came back and spoke to Samantha.

'So, Samantha, how did you find this man?'

'I saw something blue and went to look at it.'

'Did you see anybody here when you got home?'

'No, sir.'

'And any cars? Did any cars go past you on the Chapanoke Road?'

'No, sir.'

'OK. That's all, Samantha. Now, you must forget about this. I know it'll be difficult, but try.'

For years, nobody found the killer of Alvin Howell in the swamp, and for years Samantha couldn't forget.

Chapter 2   October 1989, Monday Afternoon

'Hi, Samantha, you pretty thing! We're here.'

Samantha's father's brother, Jack, and his wife, Peaches, got out of their car. Sam smiled, but she knew she wasn't pretty.

'Hi, Uncle Jack, Aunt Peaches. Where's Buck?'

Jack opened the back door of the car and Buck, a large black dog, jumped out. Jack took out two bags of dog food.

'Now, you be careful with our Buck. He's a beautiful and very expensive dog,' said Peaches. 'Give him his food three times every day, wash him every two weeks, and walk him every day.'

'Right, Aunt Peaches. He'll be OK with me.'

'I know he will. You're a good girl. Oh, think, tomorrow morning we'll be in Paris.'

Samantha didn't want to think about the next six weeks: Jack and Peaches in Europe and Africa, and she, Samantha, in North Carolina, USA, by old Powhatan Swamp. Nothing happens here . . . she thought.

Jack and Peaches left and Sam took Buck out into the garden. Suddenly, Buck sat up, looked to the right and ran. Sam looked up – there, to the right, was a big black bear, and there was Buck, running after it into the swamp.

'Buck! Come back here, you bad dog!' called Sam, but Buck didn't stop. Angry, Sam ran into the house for her shoes and jacket; she couldn't wait for Buck to come back. 'I must follow him,' she thought.

Henry, an American black bear, came from the south of the Powhatan. Born in the spring, he stayed with his mother through the winter, sleeping, then left his 'home' the next April. Now he was six years old and he was a very beautiful bear. More important, he didn't laugh or turn away from my face.

Charles Clewt, Ohio State University

There, to the right, was a big black bear.

Sam took her jacket and looked at her gun, but she didn't take it; she didn't know how to use it. She ran out of the house, hearing her mother's words from all those years ago: 'Never go into the swamp without your father or me, Samantha — never.' Well, now she must. She could hear Buck and she started to walk into the swamp.

There are about 22 different animals in the swamp, and more than 1,000 birds. The swamp is living. Sometimes I talk to it, and it talks to me.
Charles Clewt, Ohio State University

She was now near the centre of the swamp. It was four-thirty in the afternoon, and in winter the swamp was dark by five. Sam knew the sounds of the swamp — the birds, the animals, and now Buck. At quarter to five she heard a different sound — the sound of a gun. Then she heard it again. Sam wasn't afraid of guns; she was more afraid because she knew that she had only fifteen minutes before it was dark, and she didn't have a light with her. Then she understood — she was in the swamp for the night and she must find a place to sleep. She couldn't hear Buck now. Was he OK or was he dead? Bears are big animals and can easily kill dogs. Well, that was Buck's problem — hers was the night. She found an old tree and climbed into it.

♦

It was a long, difficult night. Sam didn't sleep much, and she thought a lot about the body in the swamp seven years before. By early morning, before it was light, she knew what to do: John Clewt and his son lived across Lake Nansemond, only about two miles away. She could go there and phone her mother. The son — Charles — was weird — that's what people said — a 'weirdo'. But she only wanted to use their phone.

At first light, Sam opened her eyes after a short sleep. She could hear — and see — something, someone near the tree. She wanted to call out, but something stopped her. She remembered Alvin

She found an old tree and climbed into it.

Howell again and suddenly she was very afraid. Now she could see the man – a big man, in a coat and hat, and with something in his arms – something long. She looked at the thing in his arms . . . was that a foot? Then the man walked away. Sam waited in the tree . . .

Minutes later, the man came back and walked past the tree again, but this time he didn't have anything in his arms. Again, Sam waited. After some minutes she heard the sound of a car – starting and driving away from the swamp. Then everything was quiet again.

We lived by Lake Nansemond. My father worked on the lake. Nansemond is a young lake, but it's weird. The water is red – the colour of blood.

Charles Clewt, Ohio State University

Sam walked along the side of the lake, saw the house and felt happy for the first time in more than twelve hours. She was not far from the house when she heard the sound of two dogs – oh, no! They were after her! She ran and jumped up above the door of the house, but she was too slow; one of the dogs caught her foot in its teeth. Nine o'clock in the morning, nobody at home, and now here was a worse problem than the night in the swamp!

Chapter 3   Tuesday Morning

About an hour later, Sam heard a boat on the other side of the lake. She looked out. Yes, there was a boat – it was now quite near to the house. When it arrived, someone climbed out of it and came to the house. It was Clewt's son.

'Hey, there!' called Sam.

The boy stopped

'I'm up here.'

He looked up. 'What are you doing up there?'

Sam told him about the dogs. Now he was nearer she could see his face under the hat: the right side of it was OK but the left

Sam heard a boat on the other side of the lake.

side was brown and there was something wrong with his left eye. His left ear was small and brown. Yes, his face was weird.

The boy climbed up and carried Sam down.

'What happened to your feet?' he asked.

'I walked through the swamp last night.'

'Why?'

'Oh, Buck, my uncle's dog, ran into the swamp after a bear, a big, black bear,' Samantha said.

'Mmm, I think that's Henry,' the boy said.

In the house he brought her a phone and she called her mother. When she put the phone down, he said. 'I'm Charles, but people call me Chip. Sorry about the dogs. Are you hungry?'

'Yes, I last ate yesterday afternoon.'

'OK. I'll make some breakfast.'

Chip brought the food and they talked and ate. After eating, Chip looked at Sam's feet, went into the kitchen and came back with some hot water and a bottle.

'This will help. Put your feet in the water.'

They talked about the swamp and the bears, and Sam told Chip about her night in the tree and the man. And then Sam found the words to ask: 'What happened to you?'

'I was in an accident ten years ago, a plane accident. My face is better now than it was then. But the fire was very bad . . .' He stopped and looked away.

'I'm sorry. It was wrong of me to ask,' said Sam.

Chip got the boat out to take Sam to Dunnegan's, a shop about ten minutes from the Clewts' house by boat. He gave her some of his shoes to wear and carried her to the boat, then he started talking about the bears: 'Tom – Tom Telford – and I are working with the bears. We want to find the number of bears in the swamp now. We think the number will be more now, after the ban on killing the bears four years ago. We think there are more birds, more of all the animals. The killing mustn't start again.' The

'I was in an accident ten years ago, a plane accident.'

boy stopped talking and Sam thought about her father – a hunter. He wanted the bear-hunting to start again!

◆

Soon they arrived at Dunnegan's. Chip carried Sam to a chair outside the shop. 'Will you stay and meet my mother?' she asked.

'No, I must get back.'

'Well, thanks for everything. I'll bring these shoes back soon.'

'When you're ready. See you.'

Chapter 4   May 1988

Spring in the Powhatan begins in March. Suddenly everywhere is green. The bears come out of their long winter sleep and start looking for food. Birds arrive on the lake. For me, it's the best time of the year.

Charles Clewt, Ohio State University

Eighteen months before Buck ran into the swamp after Henry the bear, Chip wasn't happy. He lived with his father by the lake, but he had nothing to do. Then, one day, Thomas Telford, a student from North Carolina University, arrived.

He was there to do some work for the university with the black bears in Powhatan and he wanted someone to help him. He asked Chip.

In early June Chip started working with Telford. On the first morning they drove into the swamp. They wanted to find the bears. Telford showed Chip their work: they made traps to catch the bears, but they didn't kill them; Telford gave each bear a number and a small radio so that they could follow the bear round the swamp and know where it went at different times of the year. Chip's accident was ten years before, and now, for the first time, he was happy again. He loved this work.

Then, one day, Thomas Telford arrived.

The next morning they went back to their traps. In one trap there was a large black bear – he was very angry.

'He's big,' said Telford. 'Wait here, I'll get the gun. Don't worry – there's no danger, he'll sleep for some minutes, then he'll be OK.'

Telford shot something into the bear's leg. First, the bear fought sleep, but soon Bear 1–88 (number 1 in 1988) went quietly to sleep. Telford started work – writing things about the bear: how big, tall, heavy he was – and then he put his number on the bear's ear and he put the radio round the animal's neck.

'Right,' said Telford. 'Now we can follow Bear 1–88. He'll get up again soon and run back into the swamp.'

'Do you give the bears names?' asked Chip.

'No, I don't,' Telford answered. 'Do you want to?'

'Yes,' said Chip, 'I think I'll call this bear Henry.'

♦

For some months Chip and Telford worked with the bears. They trapped them and followed them.

Telford told Chip about his work:

'I want to find the number of bears in the swamp. Five years ago there weren't enough bears here. That's why there's a ban on bear-hunting. When there are more bears, the ban will stop.'

'But that's wrong!' Chip couldn't understand. 'So people will come and hunt the bears again?'

'Yes, but sometimes it's right to hunt the bears. We can't have too many bears in the swamp.

Chip liked Telford a lot now and this was the first time he thought differently from him. Perhaps Telford couldn't fight the bear-hunting, Chip thought, but *he* could.

♦

One afternoon in late September, Chip and Telford heard dogs, and then they heard a gun, too. They looked up and Ethel, Bear

They trapped the bears and followed them.

number 11-88, fell from a tree, with blood on her side. She started to fight the dogs, but then the hunter saw Telford and Chip and called the dogs. He turned to the two young men and shot at them, then ran away. But it was too late – Ethel was dead.

'Do you want to follow him?' asked Chip. He wanted to cry.

'No, I saw him. I'll know him again, and I'll know that hat and red and black coat again.' Telford spoke slowly, angrily.

♦

I remember my first cold, dark, wet December in the swamp. The bears were now fat, ready for the long winter sleep with no food. I could hear some birds, but the winter swamp was usually very quiet, waiting for the spring, when it could live again.

Charles Clewt, Ohio State University

The winter came. Telford went away to visit his girlfriend and his family. Then spring came and he came back to the Powhatan. he and Chip started their work again. They worked all through the next summer and Chip was very happy. Then it was time for Telford to go back to the university again.

One Monday afternoon in October 1989 he left Chip in the swamp and started to drive back to North Carolina University. Soon after he left the swamp, he came to an old brown truck in front of him on the road. Telford stopped, angry at first, but then he was suddenly afraid; there was a black bear in the truck – dead – and a man was next to it, in a large hat and a red and black coat.

The man turned and looked at Telford. He smiled and took his gun. Telford knew this was the hunter from the swamp, a year ago. He was very afraid. The man turned his gun on Telford.

'OK, boy. Come down out of your truck now, nice and slow . . . That's right. Now, put your hands above your head . . .'

There was a black bear in the truck – dead – and a man was next to it.

Chapter 5   October 1989

Sam's mother met her at Dunnegan's and they started driving home. Sam told Dell about Buck running into the swamp (he was now back at the house!). She talked about her night in the tree, the quiet hunter in the swamp, and about Chip Clewt, the weirdo.

'That boy with the weird face?' her mother asked.

'He's very nice, Mum. He's helping Telford with the bears. He wants to keep the ban on bear-hunting in the swamp.'

Dell looked at her daughter. 'The men are talking about hunting bears again next year. Your father thinks he's going to start hunting them again. He'll soon hear about Chip Clewt and his fight for the bears – and it's better that he doesn't hear it from you. So don't see the boy again. OK?'

'Well, I'm going to take his shoes back to him.' Sam couldn't understand why she was angry about her mother's words.

♦

The next night Sam had a bad dream – again. She was afraid – it was her usual dream about Alvin Howell. She often had these dreams. She always saw the body in the blue shirt with the blood on it; she often heard Alvin ask for help. Sometimes she saw an old truck in her dreams, but she couldn't remember seeing a truck on that day when she was only nine years old

♦

Early the next week Chip had a call from Ed Truesdale, the policeman from Currituck. Truesdale was afraid for Tom.

'When did you last see him?' he asked Chip.

'Last Monday – more than a week ago.'

'Where did you see him?'

'Here, in the swamp, west of the lake. He was in his truck, ready to drive home.'

Sometimes she saw an old truck in her dreams.

'And he's not with his girlfriend now?'

'No, he didn't arrive, and he's not with his family.' Chip was also very afraid for him.

'Did he have any problems here with anybody?'

'No, we don't see many people here in the swamp, but there was one man, last year . . .' Chip told the policeman about the hunter, but Truesdale didn't think it was important.

Later, Chip started thinking about the hunter again and then remembered Sam's story about the man in the swamp. He called Sam and asked her about him.

'Sam, do you think that perhaps it was a bad dream?'

'No, it wasn't a bad dream. Everybody asks me that. I saw him. Why do you ask?'

'Because we can't find Tom. He left here last week but he never arrived at his family's home. You were in the swamp on the same night. Perhaps you can tell the police about the hunter in the swamp . . .'

◆

Later that week Sam was back at school. One day her father met her on the road home and stopped the truck.

'Hi, Sam. Get in. How was school today? How are your feet?'

'OK, Dad. How are you?'

'I'm very happy. I've got a trap for that black bear and next time he comes near our house, I'm going to kill him.'

Sam turned away, unhappy.

◆

The next Saturday morning Sam phoned Chip.

'I'd like to bring your shoes back.'

'OK. Can you walk now?'

'Yes, I went back to school on Thursday.'

'I'll meet you at Dunnegan's. What time?'

18

Sam turned away, unhappy.

'I'm looking for him in the swamp now, or for his truck. Will
you help me?'

'Half past ten?'

'I'll be there.'

Sam arrived at Dunnegan's early. When Chip got there in his boat, he told her about Telford again.

'I'm looking for him in the swamp now, or for his truck. Will you help me?'

Sam wanted to say no and walk away. She remembered her mother's words, but she looked at his face and saw how unhappy he was.

'OK, but I must be back here by quarter past one.'

They went to the house on the lake and from there they took Chip's car into the swamp. They drove through the swamp and Chip talked about the bears and the other animals there. For the first time, Sam started to be interested in the swamp.

Chip stopped the car and they started looking on foot. They left the road and walked through the trees. After about twenty minutes, Sam saw something white in the trees and called Chip. He went to look and Sam followed, afraid – she remembered the body in the swamp from years before. They got nearer and saw Telford's white truck – but he wasn't in it. Chip looked down at something and his face went very white. He was suddenly very sad.

'Look, I think this is blood,' he said.

Chapter 6   November 1989

The hunting starts in the first week of November. First, the men hunt with only their guns, but then they bring in the dogs, and that's bad. They kill about 500 bears every year in Carolina. Next year, perhaps the hunting will start again in the Powhatan, and then that number will be 600.

Charles Clewt, Ohio State University

After they found Telford's truck in the swamp, Chip and Sam told Truesdale about it. Sam started speaking: 'I think the

21

man in the swamp is perhaps the killer of Alvin Howell.'

'Alvin Howell! Why do you think that?' Truesdale asked.

'I don't know. Perhaps it's because of the dreams. I often see a truck in my dreams . . .'

'Well, we have about 3,000 trucks round here. What year? What colour?'

Sam couldn't answer.

'Samantha, thank you for telling me this, but I don't think it's very important. And Howell died years ago. I can't understand why you think it's important now.'

'Come on, Sam, let's go,' said Chip. He could see that Truesdale was a little angry.

When Chip got home he told his father about the meeting with Truesdale.

'Truesdale won't help you, then?' asked John Clewt.

'Well, it's not that, but he didn't think Sam's dreams were very important.'

'What about hypnotizing Sam?' his father asked.

'Hypnotizing her? Why?'

'Perhaps she'll remember something more about her dreams.'

♦

Some days later, Chip took Sam to the swamp again. He wanted to show her some bears, but Sam was afraid.

'My father says I mustn't go near the bears.'

'It'll be OK. I want you to see a bear in the swamp, in it's home,' answered Chip.

'I'm afraid, Chip.'

'Don't be. Stay near me and do what I say.'

They left the car and walked along a small road. Chip could see that bears used the road, and he put his radio on. They followed number 17 – a mother bear with two young babies.

'Alvin Howell! Why do you think that?' Truesdale asked.

Soon they saw her. She took some fruit from a tree and gave it to her babies.

'Her name's Eliza. Watch her with the babies.'

Sam smiled and watched the bears playing. After about five minutes, she said: 'I must be back at Dunnegan's at half past twelve. I must go, Chip. I'll be late.'

'OK. But I want to ask you a question before you go. Do you want those bears to die?' Chip asked her.

'No! What do you think I am?'

They went back to Dunnegan's in the boat. Sam talked to Chip. 'Chip, you know I don't want the bears to die, but you must be careful. You don't understand the people here – they're hunters and they're dangerous. You can't stop them. They'll stop you first, you'll see.'

'But I must stop them, Sam. I'm working with the National Wildlife Conservancy.★ It'll be in the newspaper tomorrow. Will you help me?'

'I can't, Chip. My father's a hunter. He'll throw me out of the house!'

But Chip didn't listen – now he knew that she also thought that the bears were important. Then, when they were near to Dunnegan's, he asked her something very weird . . .

'Sam, I'd like somebody – a doctor or somebody – to hypnotize you. What do you think?'

'Hypnotize me? I don't know. Why?'

'Because perhaps you'll remember more about finding Howell, and about the hunter in the swamp.'

Sam couldn't answer. Why did she listen to this weird boy?

♦

★ National Wildlife Conservancy: people working together to stop the hunting of animals.

'Her name's Eliza. Watch her with the babies.' Sam smiled and watched
the bears playing.

The next morning – Sunday – when the newspaper arrived, Sam read the story about Chip. 'Oh no!' she thought. 'What will Dad say now?'

When she went down to the kitchen, her father was on the phone: 'OK. You call five people, I'll call five people and we'll ask them to call some other people. We'll meet next week.'

He put the phone down and looked at Sam.

'That young friend of yours . . . Did you know about this?'

'About what, Dad?'

'This plan of his to stop us from hunting next year.'

Sam didn't say anything; it was better to stay quiet. Her father started talking again.

'I don't know. They'll want to stop us eating next – these people. People started to hunt because they wanted the food.

'That was years ago; people don't eat bear meat now,' Sam thought, but she didn't say anything.

The next day she went back into the swamp with Chip. He stopped the car and turned to her. 'I'd like to see the tree,' he said.

'The tree?'

'Yes, you were in a tree that night, remember?'

She showed him the tree, and again she told him about the hunter and the thing in his arms. She understood then that he thought it was Thomas Telford in the man's arms – dead – and she also understood that finding Telford's killer was very important to Chip.

◆

On Tuesday evening, Chip and his father were at the table in the kitchen. Suddenly, at twenty to nine John Clewt saw something red outside the window. Then there was the sound of a gun and the sound of the window breaking. 'Get down!' He pulled Chip from the table and under the window, the best place to be. The gun sounded again and then everything went quiet. They waited; nothing

'Did you know about this . . . this plan of his to stop us from
hunting next year.'

more happened. Chip looked at his father and saw blood on his face.

'Dad, your face . . .' he said.

His father put his hand to his face. 'It's OK,' he said.

'I think somebody wants to tell us something,' Chip said. His father didn't answer. 'How did he get here without the dogs hearing him?' he asked.

'Perhaps he came in a very quiet boat,' said Chip's father.

'Do you think this is because of the story in the newspaper?' asked Chip.

'Yes, but I don't think he wanted to kill us. He wants us to be afraid, that's all.'

'Well, I am afraid. What do we do now?'

'For tonight we stay here. The police can't do anything now; we'll call them in the morning.'

But early the next morning they had a call from Dunnegan. They always left their car outside his shop.

'Come and look at your car,' he said. 'Somebody here doesn't like you.'

At Dunnegan's they waited by the car for the police. Chip's father spoke after a minute or two.

'Chip, somebody came to the house last night and shot at us, then they came here and broke the car windows. Let's walk away from this.'

'What do you want to do?'

'Perhaps go and live in a different place. Or perhaps we can take that long holiday in Europe.'

'That's running away, Dad.' Chip looked at his father.

'Yes, I know. I don't want anything to happen to us.'

'What about the bears?'

'Chip, you and I are more important than the bears, and I don't like this – too much is happening here. First Telford, then us, now the car . . .'

Chip was quiet for a minute, then he spoke.

'Come and look at your car,' he said. 'Somebody here doesn't like you.'

'No, Dad. You go. I'll stay here. Perhaps I can live with Dunnegan.'

His father looked at him sadly. 'OK, Chip, we'll stay.'

That afternoon Dunnegan called Sam and told her about the shooting at the Clewts' house, and their car. She called Chip.

'Dunnegan told me about last night. You were lucky.'

'Well, Dad cut his face, but he's OK.'

'Chip, you cannot fight the hunters. You don't understand. They won't stop . . .'

'No, and *I* won't stop.'

'Chip, they're all working together. There's a meeting next week . . .'

'What day? What time?'

'Friday night. I don't know the time.'

'I'll go. I'll talk to them.' He was angry.

'Chip, there'll be more problems . . .'

'That's too bad.'

◆

On Thursday morning, Truesdale called and went with Chip to the Swamp. There *was* blood near Tom's truck, and he wanted to look round again. Truesdale asked again about the hunter with the dogs from the year before – perhaps it *was* important. The two went to see Jack Slade, an old hunter. They told him about Telford.

'That boy – I knew what people round here thought about him. They didn't like his work – working with the bears!'

'So you think somebody killed him – because of the bears?' asked Truesdale.

'Yes, that's what I think.'

'Mr Slade, do you know a hunter round here, a big man, wears a red and black coat and a big hat?' Chip asked.

'No, no, I don't think I do.'

There was blood near Tom's truck.

When Chip and Truesdale left, Slade went across the road and spoke to Grace Crosby in the shop.

'When you see Buddy Bailey, tell him to come and see me. It's important.'

Later that evening, before it was dark, Buddy Bailey arrived at Slade's home. 'You wanted to see me?'

'Yes, Truesdale was here today. He's asking people about that Telford boy. He's looking for somebody with a red and black coat.'

'What did you tell him?'

'Nothing, Buddy. You know me.'

'You did the right thing. Thanks, Jack. Do you want some more of that bear meat?'

'Mmm, yes. I love that bear meat of yours.'

When Buddy got home, he took his red and black coat and threw it on the fire.

Chapter 7   Nine Days

The next day Sam got home from school and knew that something was wrong. The dogs were very excited. Then she heard the bear. She put her books down and ran round to the back of the house. Then she saw it: a big black bear with its left foot in her father's trap! The bear was afraid and very weak. She ran to the house and phoned Chip.

'There's a bear in Dad's trap!'

'OK. Is it Henry?'

'I think it is. He's big.'

'OK. Slowly now. Give him some food and water, and talk to him. I'm coming now. I'll be there in about twenty minutes.'

Sam took some meat and water out to the bear, and pushed it across to him, and he sat quietly. Soon, Chip arrived.

'Yes, that's Henry. Good, he's quiet.'

Buddy took his red and black coat and threw it on the fire.

'What can you do?'

'I'm going to give him this, then he'll go to sleep and I'll take his foot out of the trap. I think he'll be OK.'

Chip took a small gun from his bag, but before he used it, they heard a truck near the house.

'Oh no! That's my father,' Sam said, and ran to meet him.

'Sam, what's that car up there?' he asked her.

'It's Chip Clewt's.'

'What's that weirdo doing here?'

'Dad there's a bear in your trap. Chip's going to get him out. I asked him to come.'

'What's wrong with you, girl!' I wanted to catch that bear. Now I'm going to get a gun and I'm going to shoot the bear, and you're not going to stop me!'

But when Sam's father arrived with the gun, she and Chip stood in front of the bear.

'Don't shoot him, Dad, please.'

'Get out of my way, Sam!'

'No, Dad. I'm not moving. You can shoot me.'

Her father looked at her sadly, then he turned round and went back to the house. Sam sat down weakly and started to cry.

'You can come back and stay with me, Sam,' said Chip.

'No, it's OK. I must go home and see him.'

◆

Sam, Chip and Truesdale were in Dr Manchester's office.

'I'm going to hypnotize you now, Sam. I'll take you back to the swamp three weeks ago.' Sam closed her eyes.

'Now, Sam, what can you see?'

'A man. He's coming nearer to me, and I'm afraid.'

'Why are you afraid?'

'I don't know. Perhaps it's because of Alvin Howell.'

'OK, Sam. Where's the man?'

'Get out of my way, Sam!'

'He's getting nearer. He's carrying something. I'm afraid!'

'Don't be afraid. We're here. What's he carrying?'

'I don't know, there's a foot ... no! It's a body.'

'Look at the man's face, Sam. Tell me about him.'

'I can't see. It's too dark and he's wearing a big hat ...'
Truesdale smiled 'yes' at the doctor.

'Now, Sam. Let's go back seven years to that day when you
found Howell. You're on the school bus, near your home, right?'

'Yes. The bus is going along Chapanoke Road. I'm getting off
the bus and ...' she stopped.

'You're getting off the bus and ...'

'... I can see a truck. It's turning out of Chapanoke Road.'

'What colour is the truck?'

'It's brown. It's a Ford. It's got ... the driver's a workman. I think.'

Truesdale stopped the doctor. 'That's OK. I think I know the
truck.'

♦

The next Friday evening, the evening of the hunters' meeting,
Sam's father was angry.

'You're coming to the meeting with me, Sam. That's all. I want
you to hear what I say.'

Sam was unhappy – she didn't want to go to the meeting.

When she arrived with her father and mother there were
about 300 people in the room. Chip was at the front. He smiled
at her. At seven-thirty her father stood up and spoke to all the
people about the bear-hunting. Sam got up and went to sit with
Chip. After her father, two or three other men spoke, and Sam
got angrier and angrier. Chip wanted her help – and she could
help him! She stood up.

'I'm Samantha Sanders. You all know my father. He's a hunter,
but I want to say that I think it's wrong to kill the bears.'

Her father looked at her. 'Sit down, Sam!' he said. But she

Chip wanted her help — and she could help him! She stood up.

didn't sit down – she looked at her father. The room was quiet . . .

After a minute or two her father looked away from her and spoke to Chip. 'OK, boy come and tell us we're all killers.'

Chip stood. He took off his hat and then, for the first time in ten years, turned and showed his face to the people in the room. He told everybody about his work with the bears and that he was ready to fight for the bears. The calls from the hunters stopped him after some minutes, and he sat down.

◆

The next day Sam was in the kitchen. Her father came in.

'Sam, I must say this to you: I don't like your plan to help the bears, but I think you did the right thing when you spoke to everyone last night in the meeting. You're a strong girl!'

From then on, Sam started to work with Chip in the swamp and she began to understand his love of the bears.

Chapter 8   February

Chip and Sam sat in the coffee shop across the road from the town meeting-room and waited to hear about the ban on bear-hunting. Truesdale came in for lunch and Chip asked him about Buddy Bailey.

'I'm sorry, but I can't do anything. We all *think* he killed Telford and perhaps Alvin Howell, but we don't *know*. What's happening across the road?'

Chip answered. 'We're waiting to hear. After lunch, they said.'

After lunch, Chip and Sam went into the meeting-room. Everybody was very quiet. A man came into the room and spoke.

'We're going to open the Powhatan from next year for the hunting of some animals . . .'

Here the hunters in the room all smiled.

Chip and Sam laughed and jumped up. The bears could live!

'... but the ban on bear-hunting will stay in place for five more years.'

Chip and Sam laughed and jumped up. The bears could live!

♦

June 1990

Chip was now back in Columbus, Ohio, in hospital again for more work on his face. From October he had a place at Ohio State University, but Sam was on the phone to him every day before then. One morning, the phone rang in the Sanders's kitchen. It was Ed Truesdale. Sam's mother called up to Sam in her bedroom.

'Sam, it's Mr Truesdale, he's coming to see us.'

Truesdale arrived and spoke to Sam.

'Sam, we've got Buddy Bailey for killing Telford and Howell. You were right.'

'But how? You didn't know ...'

'It was Jack Slade. I talked to him about fifteen times. I knew he knew something. Buddy told him about both the killings.'

'Why did he tell you?'

'I don't know – something about Buddy not giving him some bear meat ...'

♦

I saw Henry again. He was OK. He didn't remember his hours in the trap. For him, it was one more day of finding food, living, hunting ... all his days will be the same, but perhaps one day he'll be unlucky and he'll meet a man with a gun ...

I'll always remember the Powhatan. I found the bears, my father, Tom and a girl called Samantha there. But most important, I learned how to look the world in the face again.

Charles Clewt, Ohio State University

ACTIVITIES

Chapters 1–2

Before you read

1 Look at the pictures on pages 3 and 5.
  a Where does this story happen?
  b What's the dog going to do?
  c Why is the girl climbing into the tree?

2 Find these words in your dictionary. They are all in the story.
  bear blood body lake side swamp weird
  Look at the map opposite page 1. Put the words above in these sentences.
  a Chip's house is at the ..... of a ......
  b There is a large ..... between Sam's house and Chip's house.
  c Sam found the ..... of a man. He had ..... on his shirt.
  d A big black ..... came into Sam's garden.
  e Charles was different from other people – he was ......

After you read

3 In Chapter 1, who:
  a was dead in the swamp?
  b told Sam, 'You must forget about this'?

4 Answer these questions about Chapter 2.
  a Why did Sam go into the swamp?
  b What did she see when she woke up in the morning?

5 Sam went into the swamp. Was she right or was she stupid?

Chapters 3–4

Before you read

6 Think of an example of a weird person. Why do you think they are 'weird'?

7 Find these words in your dictionary.
  ban hunter neck shoot trap truck
  Now use the words to finish these sentences.
  The ..... left his ...... in the wood next to the swamp. He wanted

to catch a bear but there was a ..... on killing bears in this place. Something moved in the trees. He looked through his gun. He ..... . He ran to the bear. Suddenly he fell into a .... He broke his ..... .

After you read

8 Are these sentences right or wrong?
   a Chip had a bad car accident.
   b Tom Telford was a hunter.
   c A hunter killed a bear.
   d Tom Telford wasn't afraid of the hunter.

9 Work with another student. Have a conversation.
   Student A: You are Sam. You want to ask Chip about his face. But you don't want to hurt him. Start the conversation.
   Student B: You are Chip. Answer Sam. Tell her about your accident.

Chapters 5–6

Before you read

10 What will happen to Tom? What do you think the man in the red and black coat is going to do to him?

11 Find these words in your dictionary. Then answer the questions about them.
   dream   hypnotize
   a Look at the picture of Sam on page 17. What do you think her *dream* is about?
   b Someone is going to *hypnotize* Sam. Who? Why?

After you read

12 Who are these people?
   Alvin Howell   an old hunter
   Ed Truesdale   the body in the swamp
   John Clewt   a policeman
   Jack Slade   Chip's father

13 What happens when you hypnotize people? Would you like someone to hypnotize you? Why/why not?

Chapters 7–8

Before you read

14 Look at the picture on page 39. Why do you think Sam and Chip look happy at the end of the story?

After you read

15 Who says or writes these words?
  a 'I'm not moving. You can shoot me.' – SAM
  b 'I think it's wrong to kill the bears.'
  c 'I'll always remember the Powhatan.'

16 Chip writes at the end of the story, 'I learned how to look the world in the face again.' What does he mean?

Writing

17 You are Sam. You are in the swamp and you are looking for your uncle's dog. It gets dark. You have to stay in the swamp for a night. Write about what you do and how you feel.

18 Chip wrote about Lake Nausemond, the swamp and the bears. Look back at his writing. What did Chip think about hunting? Do you think he was right? Write what *you* think about hunting.

19 You work for the *Powhatan Press*. Write a newspaper story about the town meeting. When was the meeting? How many people were there? Who spoke? What did they say?

20 You are Chip. You are in hospital in Ohio. Write a letter to Sam. Write about your face now, and thank her for her help.